# SHINE LIGHT INTO MY DARKNESS

Australia: Evangelical Sisterhood of Mary
P. O. BOX 430, Camden NSW 2570

Canada: Evangelical Sisterhood of Mary
R.R.1, Millet, Alberta, TOC 1ZO

Germany: Evangelical Sisterhood of Mary
P. O. BOX 13 01 29, 64241 Darmstadt

UK: Evangelical Sisterhood of Mary
17 Gills Hill Lane, Radlett, Herts. WD7 8DE

USA: Evangelical Sisterhood of Mary
P. O. BOX 30022, Phoenix, AZ 85046-0022

www.kanaan.org

# Shine Light into my Darkness

## WINNING THE WAR AGAINST DESPONDENCY

M. Basilea Schlink

Evangelical Sisterhood of Mary
Darmstadt, Germany

# CONTENTS

Say to those with fearful hearts,

Be strong,
and do not fear,
for your God is coming
to destroy your enemies.
He is coming
to save you.

Isaiah 35:4 NLT

# Where is my God now?

Do you ever ask yourself: "Where is God? I can't find Him anywhere – He's like a stranger. I don't understand. Didn't He promise never to leave or forsake me? Yet He seems absent, leaving me desolate, with no way ahead and no help in sight."

That's what it feels like, but what if the reality is different? Have you ever considered that God might actually be closest when He seems furthest away? Or that when you can't understand Him, He is revealing Himself as God? God is God and not man. He is beyond human understanding, His thoughts and ways are infinitely higher than ours. He has far-reaching plans for your life; plans that are firmly anchored in His saving purposes. The very fact that you can't understand God is a sign that He is at work in your life.

"But why does life have to be so bewildering?" you ask. "Will God always be a stranger to me, remote and hard to understand? I'm in such turmoil. It's tearing me apart."

So how do you understand a God who is beyond understanding? There is a way. Even now, you can draw very close to Him – by coming as His child.

Consider the ideal father. Although a child may not follow the reasoning of adults, there is one person they will always understand – the father they love and trust. Perhaps a child needs to be disciplined, or has to go to hospital for painful treatment. The concern is to spare them greater harm to body or soul, but all the child knows is that it hurts. Yet deep down inside they do understand because they recognize their father's caring heart. Love has a way of seeing beneath the surface and discovering a person's heart. Love senses intuitively what is hidden from others. Secure in a father's affection, the child knows instinctively that the decision is in their best interests. Nothing can shake their confidence that all will be well in the end.

Become like a little child, and the kingdom of heaven is yours! This is Jesus' challenge to us. The first step is to admit the truth. What are we compared with Almighty God? Small, insignificant, limited. Does it seem as if God has led you the wrong way or is demanding too much of you? The fact is, we don't know better than our heavenly Father, any more than a small child knows better than the adults. So accept yourself for the child that you are. Be willing to honour the truth. Admit that it is foolish and presumptuous to sit in judgment over your Maker. Who are you to say His leadings are too hard to accept, or that He won't bring good out of bad situations? However deep the pain in our lives may be, there is nothing He cannot turn around for blessing.

So acknowledging the truth is the first step. The next is to respond to the Father's love with trust. God is the ultimate Father. He invented family and fatherhood (Ephesians 3:14–15). His nature can be summed up in a single word: love (1 John 4:8).

God proved His love for us by tearing His beloved Son from His heart and delivering Him up to death in order to save us from the source of all misery: sin. In His compassion He reaches out to us and loves us back to wholeness. If anyone loves us, then it is our heavenly Father.

So if you are wondering where God is in your darkness, the answer is: He is with you right now. And if you are wondering, "Why am I being singled out? Doesn't God care that I'm hurting?" – the answer is: He does. He cares enough to work in you, to correct and refine you. You matter to Him, and His aim is your happiness in all eternity.

Your part is to trust in His love.

Where is God? Right there, in your pain and darkness. Trust Him, and you will find Him – this very day. The crushing weight will lift, turmoil and despair will cease. You will know beyond all doubt that you are loved; that God has planned your path in love, and the outcome will be blessing.

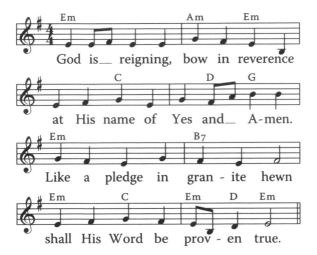

God is__ reigning, bow in reverence
at His name of Yes and__ A-men.
Like a pledge in gran - ite hewn
shall His Word be prov - en true.

God is looking down from heaven.
Will He find souls who will trust Him,
Trust Him when they feel betrayed,
Trust that God makes no mistakes?

Who can understand God's counsels,
Who is privy to His secrets?
Only love sees deeper still,
Watches God His Word fulfil.

Name of names in highest heaven,
God forever YES and AMEN.
What He says will come to pass,
and His hand we'll see at last.

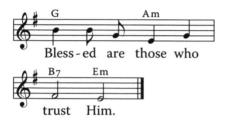

Bless-ed are those who trust Him.

15

# Honour-bound by His word

The word of the LORD is proven;
He is a shield to all who trust in Him.

Psalm 18:30 NKJV

Why am I so overwrought?
Why am I so disturbed?
Why can't I just hope in God?
Despite all my emotions,
I will believe and praise the One
who saves me and is my life.
My God, my soul is so traumatized;
the only help is remembering You
wherever I may be.

Psalm 42:5–6a VOICE

How much longer will you forget me,
LORD? Forever?
How much longer will you hide
yourself from me? …
I rely on your constant love;

I will be glad, because you will rescue
me. I will sing to you, O Lord,
because you have been good to me.

Psalm 13:1–6 GNT

When You humbled me, You did so out
of faithfulness. Now let Your unfailing
love be my comfort, in keeping with
Your promise to Your servant.

Psalm 119:75–76 VOICE

And so I am thankful and glad, and I
feel completely secure, because you
protect me from the power of death …
You will show me the path that leads
to life; your presence fills me with joy
and brings me pleasure forever.

Psalm 16:9–11 GNT

Though I walk through the valley of the
shadow of death, I will fear no evil;
for You are with me; Your rod and Your
staff, they comfort me.

Psalm 23:4 NKJV

My health may fail, and my spirit may grow weak, but God remains the strength of my heart; he is mine forever.

Psalm 73:26 NLT

Praise be to the Lord, to God our Saviour, who daily bears our burdens. Our God is a God who saves.

Psalm 68:19–20

They cried to the LORD in their trouble,
and he saved them from their distress.
He brought them out of darkness,
the utter darkness,
and broke away their chains.
Let them give thanks to the LORD
for his unfailing love
and his wonderful deeds for mankind,
for he breaks down gates of bronze
and cuts through bars of iron.

Psalm 107:13–16

Be strong and courageous. Do not be afraid; do not be discouraged,

for the LORD your God will be with you
wherever you go.          Joshua 1:9

In this world you will have trouble. But
take heart! I have overcome the world.

John 16:33

You did not receive the spirit of bond-
age again to fear, but you received the
Spirit of adoption by whom we cry out,
"Abba, Father."          Romans 8:15 NKJV

He lifted me out of the pit of despair,
out of the mud and the mire.
He set my feet on solid ground
and steadied me as I walked along.

Psalm 40:2 NLT

In the multitude of my anxieties within
me, Your comforts delight my soul.

Psalm 94:19 NKJV

God has not given us a spirit of fear,
but of power and of love and of a sound
mind.          2 Timothy 1:7 NKJV

My Father,
I do not understand You,
but I trust You.

# Hope reborn

Though darkness is all around me,
I wait for day to break.

Though I'm going through hell,
I know I am on my way to heaven.

Though deserted and alone,
I am held in the Father's embrace.

Though enticed by the tempter's voice
a thousand times,
I will not listen a single time.

Though conscious only of sin
and death within,
I live in expectation of a resurrection.

Though desolate and despairing,
I look forward to a fresh start.

Though crushed and broken, deeply
wounded, I am trusting You to love me
back to wholeness. Never, Lord Jesus,
would You abandon me to guilt
and death, for You are love, only love.

When tempted to despair,
hold on in faith.
Look up, focus on heaven.
There the crown of life
awaits you!

# Winning the war against despondency

- Pay no attention to doubts and inner turmoil.

- Trust in God's love without trying to understand Him.

- Humbly accept God's incomprehensible leadings.

- Admit that God's thoughts are higher than ours.

- Don't expect to make sense of God with your human reasoning.

- Honour God's commands and respect His holy will.

- Obey God wholeheartedly, wanting only what He wants.

- Hold on to His word of promise.

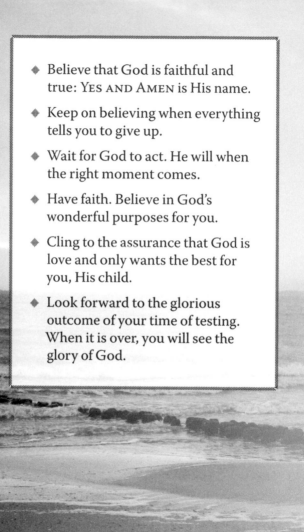

- Believe that God is faithful and true: YES AND AMEN is His name.

- Keep on believing when everything tells you to give up.

- Wait for God to act. He will when the right moment comes.

- Have faith. Believe in God's wonderful purposes for you.

- Cling to the assurance that God is love and only wants the best for you, His child.

- Look forward to the glorious outcome of your time of testing. When it is over, you will see the glory of God.

The more
you focus on
your struggles,
the more they will
pull you down.
Focus instead on
JESUS.
Walk in His freedom
and light.

# For dark moments

*You say: Night consumes my soul.*
*I am incapable of believing, praying, loving.*

Jesus says:

Then let it be night. This is the time when the false lights in your soul go out and a new day is ushered in. Purified in the night, you will be ready for Me, the Bright Morning Star, to rise in your life. Take courage and walk step by step through the night, obedient to God and His Word. Be faithful in your daily responsibilities; be faithful in prayer even if you feel nothing.

Just take the next step I show you in the darkness, and you will come one step closer to the light.

*There's no point in praying. Nothing will happen anyway.*

"According to your faith, it will be done to you." (Matthew 9:29 VOICE) Have faith that your prayers will make a difference. Have faith, keep on praying and I will act – but leave the timing to Me.

*God just seems to have forgotten me. No help, no answer, no solution to my problems in sight.*

Wait patiently for Me to step in. My help will never come too late.

*No one understands what I'm going through.*

Self-pity never helped anyone. Take your stand by declaring: "I know the One who made and saved me. He loves and understands me. At the right time He will send someone to provide understanding and support, if I only have eyes to see them."

*I don't feel like living any more.*
*There's just no point.*

> Leave it to Me to decide whether your life
> has a purpose, for just now you are not in
> a position to judge. Later, looking back,
> you will see the value of your life. Live
> each day as it comes, following wherever I
> lead with an unqualified Yes. As your will
> becomes one with Mine, your life will be
> given the deepest meaning.

*My problems and burdens are crushing me.*
*It's unbearable.*

> The moment you say, "I will take up my
> cross," your burden will become bearable.
> For the humble of heart, every burden is
> bearable. Humble yourself beneath My
> hand, and the crushing weight will lift.

*What did I do to deserve such a rough deal*
*in life? It's not fair.*

> Trust in My love and stop comparing
> yourself with others, which only fosters
> envy and self-pity. These negative atti-

tudes take you straight into the trap of the devil, who really will make life hard for you. How do you know others suffer less than you do? You can't see into their hearts. Behind the smiles and laughter there might be heartache and tears. And who knows what tomorrow might hold?

If you are going through a rough patch now, cling to the truth that I discipline those whom I love. I shape My chosen ones in the furnace of affliction, with a view to their eternal happiness. So don't compare yourself with others – give thanks for what I am doing in your life.

*I can't take any more. It's all too much.*

Shouldering your cross instead of shying away from it, you will find that My yoke is easy and My burden light (Matthew 11:30). I personally designed your cross. It's made to measure. Do you know what is actually wearing you out? Your complaining. That's why you think you can't take any more.

*I can't cope with all the demands at work.*

> Whoever you're working for, aren't I the One you want to please? I am your ultimate employer. I know what is expected of you and will enable you.
>
> Pause for a moment. Whose agenda are you following – yours or Mine? Are some of the things you are doing unnecessary? Maybe you are doing too much in your own strength, leaving Me no scope to help?

*I can't live under these circumstances, they're just too depressing.*

> Learn to see My hand in your life. You are My beloved child, and I have only good plans for you. Yes, life can be beyond understanding. Even so, I am leading you.
>
> All I ask of you is to trust Me and My perfect will. In surrender you will find peace.

*Some people are just impossible.*
*Why do I have to put up with them?*

> I am the One who brought them into your life. They are there for a purpose. Realizing you can't cope drives you to Me. Reach out for the true and lasting love that only I can give. Such love will bring you joy in this life and then glory for all eternity.

*I'm fed up. I feel like packing in.*

> If you do that, you lose the crown of glory that awaits you in heaven. It is yours only if you fight the good fight and run the race to the end.

God seeks those
who will obey Him in faith,
trusting in His love
even in the darkest of nights.

Jesus Himself endured
utter darkness in Gethsemane.
But He had a staff to lean on
as He walked through
the night.
It was the staff of obedience:
"Father, not My will, but Yours."

Follow Jesus' lead and say,
"Yes, Father",
and you will win through
in your own Gethsemane.

Walking in obedience,
you will not go wrong.

# Staying the course

As with other prayers in this book, you might find it helpful to pray this with someone you trust.


My dear Lord Jesus,

So many have deserted You in dark moments, causing You deep pain. I don't want to do that to You. Sometimes I feel trapped with no way out. It would be so easy to give up, but that's cowardly, and You deserve my wholehearted commitment. I know I've often let You down and that's reflected badly on You. But I'd rather battle on at Your side in all weakness than break Your heart by deserting when the going gets tough.

My Lord Jesus, I give myself to You. I am committed to staying the course, no matter how often I stumble. Help me to see that it's my hurt pride that makes me want to quit. Give me the courage to accept myself with all my limitations and inadequacy.

Before heaven and all the powers of hell I give You, Lord, my unconditional Yes. Yes, I am a sinner. Yes, I have failed. Yes, I have problems and burdens. But I renounce before God all negativity and defeatism, every feeling of "I want out! I can't take any more!" I take my stand on Your word: resist the devil and he must flee! Yours is the victory!                              Amen.


Submit yourselves,
        then, to God.
Resist the devil,
    and he will flee from you.
Come near to God
    and he will come near to
you ... Humble yourselves
        before the Lord,
    and he will lift you up.

James 4:7-10

# Trusting
# when all is dark

My dear Lord Jesus,

In me is darkness, but You are light,
pure light without a trace of darkness.

In me is sadness,
but in You is undying joy.

In me is sin and guilt,
but in You is sinlessness.
And Your righteousness is mine,
for I belong to You.

In me is hopelessness and confusion,
but knowing You have a purpose in
everything is enough for me.

In me all is dead and lifeless, but You
are life; and what is Yours is mine.

You let me go through hell, but only
that I may taste heaven.

You lead me through spiritual night
and death, but only to shower me with
the blessings of Your restoring love.

You let me become painfully aware
of my weakness and sin,
but only so that I will taste the fullness
of Your mercy and salvation.

My one desire is to gladden Your heart
by looking to You for everything.
For me it is enough to know that You
love me and are always there.

Amen.

# Faith

Faith shines brightest at night; its beams reach furthest in the dark.

True faith is strong, expecting nothing of self but everything of the God who makes the impossible possible.

Faith is shot through with joy. Joy at what God is going to do. Joy in the assurance of His help. Joy in anticipation of victory.

Faith always wins in the end. With the almighty God on our side, we will never be defeated.

# Worn down by worry

Loving Father,

Worry is wearing me down. My thoughts are going round and round in circles. Help me, Lord, I can't see a way out. The difficulties and unresolved issues are piling up. The burden of responsibility is crushing me. I can't break through to joy.

But I'm not going to give in to my worries. I'm not going to act as though You don't exist. Father, You know exactly what I'm going through and already have help in store. My eyes are fixed on You, for You are my sole confidence, and I have Your word that "mountains melt like wax before the LORD" (Psalm 97:5). So I will confront my anxieties head on with Your promise. You will not fail to help, for I am Your beloved child. All these mountains I see looming ahead You will cast into the sea. All power is Yours. You are always greater than my problems, and nothing can shake my confidence in You.

Jesus, Lord of life, just as You changed water into wine, You change sorrow into joy. Speak one word, Lord, and difficulties will be resolved: a way will open up where there is none. I will be comforted in my suffering and come through the other side rejoicing in Your victory. I know You are only disciplining me for my good: all you ask of me is to accept this painful path.

I am committed to bearing my cross, the yoke You have laid upon me. I am ready to face what I fear most, knowing that anxiety will then yield. Loving Father, I humble myself beneath Your mighty hand, confident that whatever You bring into My life is good – even if it comes in the form of pain and suffering.

What more could I want? I am trusting You for a miracle – whether You choose to lift me out of this crisis or to sustain me in it. Whatever happens, I can count on Your help.

Amen.

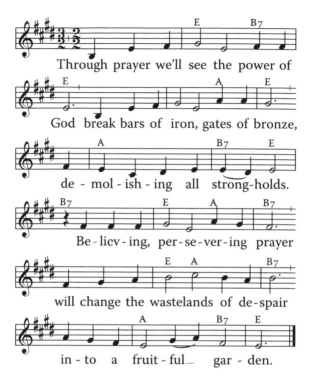

Through prayer we'll see the power of
God break bars of iron, gates of bronze,
de - mol - ish - ing all strong-holds.
Be - liev - ing, per - se - ver - ing prayer
will change the wastelands of de-spair
in - to a fruit - ful_ gar - den.

Believing prayer will move the Lord
To help His children when they call,
Appealing to His mercy.
For what could be impossible
To the almighty Lord of all,
Who made the earth and heavens?

Believing, persevering prayer
Works miracles for those who dare
To put their faith in God's Word.
Mountains like wax will melt away,
Opponents suddenly give way,
Walls of resistance crumble.

So take your stand upon God's Word.
It is a rock, a refuge sure.
His promise will be honoured.
Oh, raise the victory shout in faith,
Lift high your banner day by day,
The evil one defeating.

# I can't take any more

Lord Jesus,

Please help me. I can't take any more. I can't drown out the persistent voice in my mind: "It's not working. Give up, get out. Leave your job, your ministry, your marriage and family – whoever you can't get on with. It's killing you."

But I only want to do what You want, Lord. I know going my own way in disobedience would end in disaster.

Help me to hear what You are saying.

*I planned this time of testing especially for you, measuring it carefully so it would not be too hard. I want you to grow spiritually and become resilient. The purpose of difficult relationships is to teach you to love and not grow weary, to be gracious and not retaliate, but seek to win over the other person.*

*Bear this refining process with patience. Let suffering do its work in you. It is all part of My plan to remake you in My image, so others will see My love reflected in you. And as an overcomer you will receive the victor's crown in heaven.*

44

*So right now you find yourself in the school of suffering. Surely you don't want to leave in the middle? Do you realize that by running away from your cross you would be running away from Me? And ending up worse off than before? You can't run for ever.*

*In love I ask you: don't you want to be My disciple any more? Think of the path of pain I walked for you to Calvary, and follow closely in My footsteps. Remember the words of scripture: "We count as blessed those who have persevered"* (James 5:11). *So persevere until I lift you out of the crucible, transformed – to your joy and Mine.*

Lord Jesus, yes, I will obey Your word. I am committed to following You to the end.      Amen.

Persevere, battle on.
          Life is soon over,
but you will have all eternity
to rejoice in the fruit
          of your struggles.

Keep going,
follow the path
to the end
and see your
suffering transformed.
Paths of obedience
end in light.

47

# Breaking free
# from the death wish

My Lord Jesus,

Help me! I am in despair. Despondency, like some dark force, is taking over my life and squeezing out all hope. I am being sucked into a pit of darkness. The evil one is after me. He keeps drip-feeding me with thoughts of ending it all. He is wearing down my resistance.

So I cry to You, Lord Jesus. You are stronger than the enemy of my soul. You are the Prince of Life. You have conquered death and the death wish. Hallelujah! The prince of death has lost his hold over me, for I belong to You, the One who destroyed the power of death. Lamb of God, Your precious blood covers me. The evil one must yield; he has lost all legal right to me. At Calvary You defeated Satan, death and hell and paid my ransom price.

I renounce all the dark thoughts swirling around in my mind and the demonic powers behind them. I bind myself to You, Lord Jesus.

I am committed to obeying Your will. And it is Your will that I live and face life.

I choose life. For love of You I am ready to face suffering, knowing You love me and gave Your life for me. You would never crush me; You have help in store for every situation, no matter how hopeless.

To this I cling in faith, and so break free from these dark powers. They are determined to drive me to death: into the realm of the prince of death, who wants me as his trophy. But You have conquered him, Lord Jesus. You have rescued me, paying my ransom price. You have called me to live in Your kingdom of joy and glory for all eternity. Amen.

# Challenging
# our negative mindset

*Life is just too hard. I don't want to live any more. I'm at breaking point.*

Challenge such thoughts head on. When the pressure is on, do I throw in the towel? Or do I face up to it and trust God for a way through?

Life can be hard at times. But no struggle – no victory. God wants us to know joy for time and all eternity, free from the tyranny of sin and despair. So bear tough times bravely, trusting God to do His refining work in you. It's not for ever: there is light at the end of the tunnel.

You may be tempted to run away from hardship, only to find it catches up with you, either in this life or the next. The end-times will bring suffering on an unprecedented scale. But by turning away from God, you play into the hands of Satan, who is out to torment you. At present you are in the hands of your loving Lord and Saviour Jesus Christ, who has weighed your cross to ensure it is not one ounce too heavy

(Francis of Sales). So commit yourself to your cross. You can trust the Good Shepherd to guide you safely through the dark valley. He loves you.

Never say, "I can't take any more. My cross is just too heavy to bear. Life is too much for me."

Send Satan packing by saying Yes to God. Affirm before the unseen world: "I choose to walk the way of the cross with Jesus. My Saviour went through agony for me. How can I refuse to follow Him when the going gets tough?"

It was through suffering that Jesus entered glory (Luke 24:26) and now reigns as King of kings. Suffering was His lot in life – shouldn't it be part of our life too? The servant is not above his master. As sinners we need our share of hardship to help transform us and prepare us for heaven. In His love Jesus will walk this path with us. He went through the depths of suffering in order to help us face our own.

*Here I am, Lord Jesus. I am Yours. I turn away from despair and will stand firm to the last, trusting in Your love, which always wins.*

*Amen.*

# Gold tested by fire

Do not throw away your confidence;
it will be richly rewarded.   Hebrews 10:35

So be truly glad. There is wonderful
joy ahead, even though you must
endure many trials for a little while.
These trials will show that your faith is
genuine. It is being tested as fire tests
and purifies gold – though your faith
is far more precious than mere gold.
So when your faith remains strong
through many trials, it will bring you
much praise and glory and honour on
the day when Jesus Christ is revealed
to the whole world.   1 Peter 1:6–7 NLT

Consider it pure joy, my brothers and
sisters, whenever you face trials of
many kinds, because you know that the

testing of your faith produces perseverance. Let perseverance finish its work
so that you may be mature and com-
plete, not lacking anything.     James 1:2–4

Blessed is the one who perseveres under trial because, having stood the test,
that person will receive the crown of
life that the Lord has promised to those
who love him.     James 1:12

# Joy comes with the morning

Letter to a spiritual daughter facing inner battles

*My dear daughter,*

Thank you for sharing your heart with me. What you wrote moved me deeply. You are facing so many testings, and I want you to know that my loving thoughts are with you on this dark stretch of the way. I am praying that you won't get bogged down but will walk on bravely, close at Jesus' side. Be assured of His love. As surely as day follows night, God's paths will lead you out into the open – into light and joy, not sorrow and darkness.

The following verse has been in my heart for you: "We count as blessed those who have persevered. You have heard of Job's perseverance and have seen what the Lord finally brought about. The Lord is full of compassion and mercy" (James 5:11). Here you have a vision of the Father-heart of God and a promise to hold on to. He has prepared a wonderful outcome for you, as He did for Job. After bewilderment, tragic loss and mental anguish, Job was showered with blessings. That is God's way. Rich in mercy, full of compassion, He feels our pain with us. He submits us to the refining fire, only to bless us abundantly for all our suffering.

Isn't that comforting? Do you catch the joyful sense of expectancy? Your task now is to focus on your heavenly Father. Keep saying, "Abba, dearest Father, rich in mercy, full of compassion." Focusing on yourself and your difficulties is forbidden territory, because it is enemy territory. If you don't want the evil one to overwhelm you and drag you off to his realm of darkness and despair, don't yield to the slightest thought of discouragement. Don't accept his hand: take Jesus' hand instead. Praise Him for His love. He will always help you.

As I was praying for you, another verse came to mind: "Let us hold unswervingly to the hope we profess, for he who promised is faithful" (Hebrews 10:23). Hope is your anchor. Put your hope in what awaits you, not just in this life but also in the heavenly glory. Trust in His love as you walk the path of suffering. Keep your eyes on the goal of heaven. Things are pretty tough right now, but it will all be over one day. What will last for ever is the fruit of this time of testing. Be encouraged, my dear daughter. Let no path be too steep for you. It's worth it. Think of the City of God, where you will reign with Him one day.

So keep going. It is only because He loves you that He is leading you through the dark – to make you fit for heaven, where your reward will be glory. Remember, you are never alone. He is there to help you.

May the Lord in His wonderful love bless you with the grace to persevere in faith, to prove your love and commitment to Him when all is dark, and to honour Him with implicit trust.

*With my love and prayers,*
*Mother Basilea*

How He will help,
I do not know,
but that He'll help
I know for sure.

# Overcoming apathy

Lord Jesus,

I feel so empty and dead. No spark of life. No fire and passion for Your kingdom. No longing to spend myself for what matters to You. "Ask and it will be given to you" is what Your Word says. So I come to You, the source of life.

Death has no dominion over me. On the cross, You fought with death and won so that eternal life can be mine. And what is life but love and commitment to You and Your kingdom?

Bind me now to You. Help me to follow Your path of sacrificial love in everyday life, dying to sin and self so that life and love can spring up. It's not about me, it's about You, and being all out for the concerns of Your heart. Life comes from dying to self, because You rose from the dead. This I believe.

Amen.

# Trapped

*You say: I feel trapped in a black pit and can't get out.*

> Jesus says:
> Hold out your hand to Me, I will pull you out! Remember, I rose from the grave; I conquered sin and death.

*I see no way ahead.*

> But I do, and I have already opened it up for you! Trust Me.

*I'm stuck in a rut, nothing will ever change.*

> Don't you know what I said? "Behold, I make all things new." Whose words count, yours or Mine?

*However hard I try, it's no use – I keep falling into the same sin.*

> Don't say it's no use. That implies My victory at Calvary was no use and Satan won. Saying it's no use plays into his hands.

Proclaim the truth that I won the victory on the cross. Take your stand on My words, "It is finished!" Then My victory will be worked out in your life – in My good time.

*Not even You can help me, Lord Jesus. I'm hopeless.*

I love hopeless cases. That's where My work of salvation is best demonstrated. So rejoice in your weakness. Those who feel their weakness the most need Me the most and will receive the fullness of My blessings.

*I have such complex needs. What works for others doesn't work for me.*

Perhaps. But I make allowances for that. I'm especially there for anyone who feels disadvantaged. The greater your struggle, the more My victory will be evident in your life. Ransomed and transformed, you will be among the most costly jewels in My crown – outshining others.

*My faith has run dry.*

> Look at Me, crucified for you, and proclaim who I am: your risen Lord, Prince of Victory and Bondage-Breaker. By saying this, you are already expressing faith, even if you can't feel anything.

*God seems so far away – like a stranger.*
*I feel as if I don't really know You, Jesus.*

> First, know yourself. The more you see yourself as you really are – a sinner in need of grace – the more you will come to know Me in My love and compassion, in My victory over sin. That will bring you close to My heart.

*Jesus, I feel so flat and empty,*
*devoid of love for You.*

> Be comforted. Admitting your emptiness is the first step and will bring you the gift of My love. Reach out for it in faith. Trust in My promise of blessings for those who are painfully aware of their need.

*Why should You even bother with me?*
*I'm no good and never will be.*

Pray for a contrite, broken heart. Pray that you will fall under the conviction of sin. That is a prayer I always answer, and in your neediness you will know My loving embrace.

*I imagined it all – my whole life of faith,*
*all my praying and loving has been*
*pretence: it was all a lie.*

If that's how you feel, then it's good to face it. That's the first step towards a fresh start. The next step is believing that I can actually make all things new in your life – and allowing Me to. Getting real in your life of faith and prayer is a life-long process. So don't expect it to happen overnight. It takes humility to wait for growth and maturity.

*You did everything for me, Jesus. But what if I have ruined everything for You?*

Then take the next step and simply admit that you have ruined everything. Admit that the fruit of My redemption isn't evident in your life. No sooner have you done this than the first fruit is there – your honest confession! That will open the way for Me to help you.

*I've missed so many chances.*
*It's too late now.*

As long as you are alive, grace is available for you. Each new day is an opportunity to turn from sin. Start by being grateful instead of complaining. The grace I extend to the humble and contrite of heart can even work retrospectively, redeeming the past and restoring what has been destroyed by sin. Before you is a wide open door. Walk through it. I will be there to help you.

65

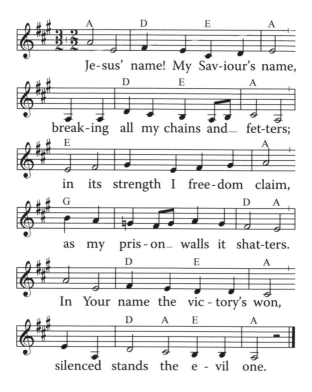

Je-sus' name! My Sav-iour's name,
break-ing all my chains and— fet-ters;
in its strength I free-dom claim,
as my pris-on— walls it shat-ters.
In Your name the vic-tory's won,
silenced stands the e - vil one.

# Change my stone-cold heart

Holy Spirit,

I cry out to You, because I'm incapable of helping myself. My heart is stone-cold and unyielding. I don't feel sorry about my sins. I react defensively when my mistakes are pointed out. Even if I know deep down I am in the wrong, I still can't admit it, I'm still unrepentant.

Holy Spirit, I am calling out to You, trusting in Your power. Creator Spirit, You call into existence things that are not: bring about in me the repentance I lack. Life-giving Spirit, quicken my soul so that I can weep over my sins and rejoice to know I am forgiven. Come to my aid. By Your creative power, soften my hard heart and make it sensitive.

Thank You, Holy Spirit, that I can count on Your help. I take my stand on Jesus' words, "How much more will your Father in heaven give the Holy Spirit to those who ask him!" (Luke 11:13).

Amen.

No more de - spond - en - cy, no more de - spair, the on - slaughts of Sa - tan will get him no - where. He flees at the might - y name of Je - sus, he flees at the might - y name of Je - - - sus.

# Renouncing accusing thoughts

Lord Jesus,

I call upon You to set me free from my negative thoughts and feelings. You see my desire to be proved right. You see how I cling to perceived hurts, convinced that I have been hard done by. You see my anger at others for failing to meet my needs. I am tormented by these accusing thoughts. They keep me awake at night.

Jesus, You are the light and the truth. Turn Your spotlight on me. Help me not to take the easy way out by blaming others. Show me the sin in my own heart that makes me resent their behaviour. Show me where I have been touchy, demanding, jealous and quick to take offence. Uncover any double standards in my life, where I expect of others what I don't live up to myself.

Above all, give me a vision of Yourself on the cross. You gave Your life for me, and what have I given You in response? So often I have failed to give You the love and honour You deserve, failed to walk in Your steps as a true disciple.

I now renounce every toxic, accusing thought from the pit of hell. Even if these thoughts come back a hundred times over, I will renounce them every single time. Lord Jesus, You are greater than all this! Your cross is the sign of victory. Accusing thoughts have lost their hold over me. To You I surrender my grievances, my supposed rights and selfish demands. You love me, and that's enough.

Jesus, Lamb of God,
I want to follow You.
Teach me to deny self,
choosing to bear
in love what
I find so hard.
Where You go,
I will go.

Amen.

Jesus, You fought and won, conquered
the e-vil one out to de-stroy my
soul. Fa-ther, I'm still Your child,
though sin flares up with might,
cours-ing like fire in my veins.

In Jesus I abide,
Safe in His wounded side.
What can the devil do?
Here is my hiding-place,
Here is redeeming grace,
Here demons dare not intrude.

71

Captain of heaven's hosts,
You overthrew the foe,
Silenced the devil's claims.
Hell lies in disarray,
Sin can no more hold sway,
Nailed to the cross of my Lord.

All this You did for me,
All this to set me free,
Nothing too hard for You.
All powers before You bow,
Sin's power within my soul,
For You are Lord, You alone.

Sing of the Lamb of God,
Sing of His precious blood,
Sing of redemption won.
Lord, have Your way in me,
Dying brings victory.
What I believe I will see.

# Shine out of me

Lord Jesus,

Help me! I just can't bear the thought of humiliation. You know how it hurts to be put down. You see how my pride rises up in protest at losing face before others. Everything in me cries out to be loved and valued, noticed and appreciated.

You alone have the power to break in me every form of pride, the desire to impress. You alone can set me free from preoccupation with self – "What do people think of me? What are they saying?" On the cross You won for me Your own humility. In faith I take my stand on Your word of victory at Calvary, "It is finished!" Sin and self have no power over me.

In the strength of Your victory, I choose to accept all that comes from Your hand of discipline, Your hand of love. By nature I would shy away in fear, but now I ask You to burn away my pride in Your refining fire. Humble me until I am truly humble and You shine out of me – to Your glory and to the joy of others. I long to be Your dwelling-place, and You have promised to dwell in the humble of heart.        Amen.

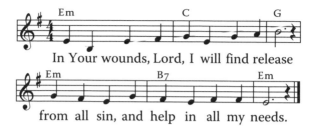

In Your wounds, Lord, I will find release

from all sin, and help in all my needs.

To this day Your blood has power divine;
New life and redemption will be mine.

In the cross I have the victory
Over Satan's evil strategy.

Crying, "It is finished!", You proclaimed
My salvation through Your bitter pain.

And Your Easter triumph is the sign
Overwhelming victory will be mine,

And Your empty grave a guarantee
That a new day soon will dawn for me.

Through Your bitter death You paved the way
For my soul to enter heaven's gates.

All this You have done for us, O Lord,
Through Your holy, precious,
                              outpoured blood.

75

# Integrity check

Have you been taking your struggle against sin seriously? Do you really want to be free?

Then make no concessions to your weak points. Don't enter into a pact with sin. Don't try to hide your vulnerability from your mentor or anyone you are accountable to. Be open with them, especially when you are really struggling with temptation.

Are you willing to admit that you are too weak on your own, incapable of freeing yourself from the sins that overpower you?

Then look for allies to join you in the battle, and be thankful for all the spiritual support you receive. By being accountable to someone you trust, you expose Satan's strategies. Accountability might include handing over anything that could be a snare. It could be money you are liable to spend on the wrong things. Or anything that is a source of temptation to you. Anything that strengthens an unhealthy or sinful relationship, for example.

Only the truth can set you free. Come into the light and own up to the un-varnished facts about your sinful habits or addictions, in the presence of a mature Christian. That is true humility, and God gives grace to the humble – and the assurance of His help.

# According to your faith

Release from chains of sin will come according to your faith. What you believe is what you will experience – nothing more and nothing less.

Do you believe that anyone who calls upon the name of Jesus will find help and deliverance? Do you believe that God can shatter bronze doors and cut through chains of iron? Do you believe that He can break the shackles that bind you?

What you believe will happen – but leave the timing to God. Waiting is humbling. But if we persevere in the battle of faith against sin, release will come. God is YES and AMEN; He does what He says. And as our loving Father He will never fail us.

But if you lose faith in God's ability to free you from slavery to sin, release will never come. Unbelief can actually be a cover-up: deep down inside we don't want to be set free. A prisoner desperate for deliverance will clutch at any human assurance of release. How much more should we trust in God our Redeemer. He is not a human who lies or goes back on his word: God keeps His promises.

Are you desperate for release from slavery to sin? Then it's better to die believing than lose the battle through unbelief. Quitting dishonours God. Persevering honours Him. Remember, no one who hopes in Him will ever be put to shame (Psalm 25:3).

Have faith,
and you will overcome.
Have faith,
and everything will change.

Times of testing
are times of growth,
birthing something new
for the Kingdom of God.

# Yes, Father —
# the key to release

Release from sin comes as we accept the discipline of the cross instead of running away from pain. Sinful desires and emotional cravings will lose their hold as you practise denying self. But if you keep choosing the easy way out, hankering after relief and numbing the pain with illicit pleasures, you will never be free.

The way to freedom is to say Yes to God and to the cross He has brought into your life. Perhaps you suffer from health issues, bad nights or loneliness. Perhaps you feel humiliated, inadequate or worthless. Whatever it is, say "Yes, Lord", and you will see the evil one yield. Say Yes, and you will gain the victory.

Let's face it. Why do we find it so hard to accept our cross? Perhaps we think we don't really need it. But as sinners we do. The heavenly Father disciplines every child of His (Hebrews 12:6). The burdens He places on our shoulders are a chance to die to sin and self. So admit that as a sinner you need the discipline of the cross.

Pampering our cravings is escapism. Take that route and you'll end up trapped in a blind alley. The key to release is to pray, "Yes, Father".

Jesus won this freedom for you, robbing Satan of his power. So take care not to hold on to your sinful desires, or you will find yourself holding on to the devil, who won't let go.

You can choose to accept the freedom Jesus won for you: it's yours for the asking. Jesus came to destroy the works of the devil. And you have His promise, "If the Son sets you free, you will be free indeed" (John 8:36).

# Victory in the name of Jesus

Lord Jesus,

You wrestled and agonized in prayer so that we could have victory. And we can claim Your victory for ourselves as we fight the good fight of faith.

I am counting on Your victory becoming a deeper reality in my life. Thank You for Your all-powerful name, a sword I can wield day by day in this battle. Help me never to grow weary, never to give up the fight, no matter how often I fall back into the same sin.

Show me the only real sin – unbelief that despairs of ever winning through. Lost battles there will be, but not a lost war, for You are fighting at my side.

Jesus, You have conquered sin and Satan, and I'll keep on calling upon Your name. Faced with my sin and the devil's power, I'll fix my eyes on You and declare with my lips who You are: the all-conquering Prince of Victory.

Amen.

My risen Saviour and Bondage-Breaker,
Your power to save I claim in faith.

My risen Saviour and Bondage-Breaker,
You shed Your blood to ransom me.

My risen Saviour and Bondage-Breaker,
Oppression lifts and I am free.

My risen Saviour and Bondage-Breaker,
At Your feet Satan conquered lies.

My risen Saviour and Bondage-Breaker,
You'll never fail my hope in You.

My risen Saviour and Bondage-Breaker,
Now sings my soul, Your victory's mine.

85

# Insights gleaned

Seeing who God is – our great and loving Father. And seeing who I am – a mere human who presumed to argue with my Maker.

Learning to humble myself like Job before the all-wise and all-knowing God and to submit to His plans and purposes.

Learning the true meaning of faith and bringing God glory by trusting when all is dark.

Learning to understand God with the wisdom of hindsight. Times of testing bring a revelation of His heart.

Loving and trusting God as never before.

Jesus, name of saving grace,
Of redemption fully paid,
Cleansing us from all our stains,
Silencing the devil's claims:
Name above all names on earth
And throughout the universe.

Jesus, name of brilliant light
Putting Satan's hordes to flight,
Blessèd be Your holy name
With its strength and power to save,
Mighty shield to ward off blows,
Driving off the fiercest foes.

Jesus, blessèd, saving name
Blotting out our guilt and shame,
Overcoming sin's control,
Quelling fears and making whole.
Jesus, name of majesty,
Heavenly authority.

Jesus, Jesus, Prince of Peace,
Mediator, Mercy-Seat,
Jesus, Jesus, Lamb of God,
Saving us upon the cross,
Cancelling our guilt and debts,
Bringing us the Father's grace.

# It's worth it!

In all your trials, never lose sight of the goal. Fight the good fight of faith to the end whatever the cost. It's worth it!

The Mount of Olives, scene of Jesus' agony as He fought with the powers of hell, became the scene of His triumphant ascension to heaven.

When your personal battle is fought and won, heaven's glory will be revealed to you – here and now. And in the life to come, a victory wreath awaits all who have stood the test.

Our lives will be crowned with glory as His was, for through suffering He opened the way to heaven. The greater the struggle, the greater the glory.

# APPENDIX

*Other literature by M. Basilea Schlink*

## FATHER OF COMFORT
Daily reflections on the God who cares, 160 pages

Through this book I came to understand and know my Heavenly Father much better – the only father I have ever known. USA

## MORE PRECIOUS THAN GOLD
Daily readings, 416 pages, hard cover

As I read the portions daily I get new joy and strength and I grow more and more spiritually. Uganda

## SOWN IN WEAKNESS, RAISED IN GLORY
From the spiritual legacy of Mother Basilea Schlink, 168 pages, large format, hard cover, full colour

During a time of turmoil and heartache I was so grateful to have this book by my side. I was comforted and upheld when it seemed that Satan was doing his utmost to drag me down in despair. Britain

## MY ALL FOR HIM   160 pages
Every time I read it, my love for Jesus is kindled. India

**BEHOLD HIS LOVE**   216 pages, hard cover

Reading it has been like going on a pilgrimage. A challenging but deeply rewarding experience. As I walked in spirit with Jesus from Gethsemane to Calvary, I saw myself in all the major players of the Passion. I felt with Him the pain. I saw into His heart. And I was awed by the love that nothing, literally, nothing could kill.                                        Britain

**KEEPING IN TOUCH WITH GOD**

80 pages, 22 colour photos

Exquisite in every way, so deeply touching, so full of the spirit of praise and faith and trust beyond measure.                                        Republic of Ireland

My friend has asked me to thank you for the book. It is like a "special friend" to her and she keeps it close to her all the time.                                        Britain

**READY WHEN THE MASTER CALLS –
THE STORY OF SISTER ANDREA**

by the Evangelical Sisterhood of Mary, 80 pages

I read it in a single day and was fascinated by Jesus' unconditional love, which comes across so powerfully. It is so down-to-earth, relevant and realistic – encouraging for ordinary people like myself.

Indonesia